Scarves
in the round

25 Knitted Infinity Scarves, Neck Warmers, Cowls, and Double-Warm Tube Scarves

Heather Walpole

Copyright © 2015 by Heather Walpole

Published by
STACKPOLE BOOKS
5067 Ritter Road
Mechanicsburg, PA 17055
www.stackpolebooks.com

Printed in the United States of America

10 9 8 7 6 5 4 3 2 1

First edition

Cover design by Wendy A. Reynolds
Photography by Heather Walpole
All photos taken in Oceanside, California.

ISBN 978-0-8117-1486-0

Cataloging-in-Publication Data is on file with the Library of Congress.

To Thomas,
Thank you for giving up knitting so
I could have a chance at it.

Contents

Acknowledgments   ix

Introduction   xi

Basic & Beautiful   1

Super Simple Cowl   2

Color Pop Cowl   5

Del Mar Derby Wrap   8

Date Night Infinity Loop   11

Sea Glass Cowl   15

Adorned   18

Basket Case Infinity Scarf   21

Lovely Lace   25

A Touch of Glitter Cowl   26

Save the Sunset Neck Warmer   30

Beach Break Loop   33

Changing Tides Cowl   36

Seaside Lace Capelet   39

Cables, Twists & Bobbles   43

High Speed Cable Cowl   44

Sweater Weather Scarf   47

Tangerine Twist   50

Double Agent Wrap   53

Popcorn & Purls   57

Entrelac Effect Neck Warmer   60

Cozy Colorwork — 65

Pixel Perfect — 66

Desert Dreams — 69

Snow Drifter Scarf — 72

Blue Lagoon Infinity Scarf — 76

The Harlequins — 79

Pretty Preppy — 82

Color Block Scarf — 85

How to Use This Book — 89

Yarn — 89

Abbreviations — 90

Gauge — 90

Blocking — 91

Techniques & Stitches — 93

Joining to Work in the Round — 93

Cable Cast-On — 94

Picot Cast-On — 95

Picot Bind-Off — 96

Cables — 97

Right Cross — 99

Bobbles — 100

Double Yarn Over — 101

Stranded Knitting — 102

Provisional Cast-On — 103

Kitchener Stitch — 105

Yarn Sources — *107*

Visual Index — *108*

Acknowledgments

Many, many thanks to:

- My sample and test knitters. Without them, the patterns in this book would not be what they are today. I am so thankful for these women, their love, feedback, and incredible knitting ability!
- My sister, Nancy Queen, who is the reason I knit. I can't thank her enough for teaching me to knit and crochet and for insisting that I keep at it even though my first few projects didn't look so hot. She has guided me on my knitting and garment design journey and it's been a fun ride!
- My mother-in-law, Pauline Walpole, who is my best cheerleader. She dreams up ideas, knits like the wind, and smiles the entire time. Her consistent check-ins helped keep me on track and kept me excited during the long road of writing a book.
- Marsha Wenskay, who has taught me more about life through knitting than ever imaginable. She showed me the calming effects of those two clicking needles and feel of the fiber running through my fingers. Her help, great ideas, and laughter motivated me more than she can know.
- Stephanie Steinhaus. She and I became fast friends through the yarn industry. We like the same colors and find the same things funny. Her endless support of Ewe Ewe Yarns and me is incredible and flattering.
- My friend Meaghan Schmaltz—we hit it off when we met on a yarn crawl. I liked her necklace and she liked my yarn. Soon we were knitting together each week and her knitting ambitions gave me new interest in our hobby. Meaghan loves to show me a new technique or point out how I've messed one up and I love that she keeps me on my toes!
- Donna Pelzar, who is the best test knitter I know. Her attention to detail is unmatched and her knitting is impeccable. It's no wonder they call her Knitting Doc Donna!
- And last but not least, my friend Jane Day. Jane doesn't know how to knit but she sure knows how to make things look good! She worked tirelessly gathering clothes and friends to style for the photographs in this book. Her eye for detail and color is unmatched and I feel like I never would have been able to complete the photos without her! We drove around Oceanside finding murals and fun buildings to make this book pop. I'll never forget our crazy time together laughing as we tried to pull off a scarf book in the August heat of Southern California.

Introduction

A scarf is probably the first thing a knitter learns how to make, usually with a pair of knitting needles. But knitting in the round is one of my favorite techniques, so what to do? Design a collection of neckwear all knit on circular needles, of course! It includes cozy cowls, infinity scarves that you can wear long or double or triple wrap, lacy capelets, and tailored neck warmers. But no classic long scarves, you ask? They're included as well, in a new form that I love—open-ended tube scarves, which are super warm. Cables, bobbles, basketweave, colorwork, lace, or just plain knit and purl, you'll find a technique and look to suit your style.

If you've never knit in the round before, no worries. In Techniques & Stitches, you'll find photo tutorials for how to join to work in the round, as well as for different types of cast-ons, bind-offs, and specific stitches called for in my patterns.

So pick a pattern, cast on, and get busy knitting yourself in circles!

Basic & Beautiful

Begin with basics. In this section there's nothing but knits and purls. These simple projects are designed to let the yarns shine through. In no time you'll have a scarf you're proud of and really want to wear. Most of the projects are knit on big needles with smooth yarns so you can see your stitches clearly. Let's keep it easy and fun, grab your needles, and cast on!

Super Simple Cowl

All you need to know is how to do a knit stitch to make this cozy cowl. Worked in a super bulky yarn on size 15 needles, it knits up in no time. Make sure to cast on and bind off loosely to ensure flexible edges; a larger needle can help for those steps.

FINISHED MEASUREMENTS
Height: 12"/30.5 cm
Circumference: 40"/102 cm

YARN
Outer by Spud & Chloë, super bulky weight #6 yarn (100% wool;
    60 yds./55 m, 3.5 oz./100 g per skein)
2 skeins #7209 Cedar

NEEDLES AND OTHER MATERIALS
- US 15 (10 mm) 24"/61 cm circular needle
- Stitch marker
- Yarn needle

GAUGE
8 sts x 13 rnds in St st = 4"/10 cm square

Directions

Loosely cast on 90 stitches. Place stitch marker and join to work in the round, being careful not to twist the cast-on stitches.

Rnd 1: Knit.

Repeat Rnd 1 until piece measures 12"/30.5 cm from cast-on edge or until desired length.

Bind off loosely.

Weave in yarn ends. Block cowl.

Color Pop Cowl

This design couples a color change with a round of purl stitch in a sea of stockinette for big impact. By choosing two neutral shades, black and gray in this case, the neon green really makes a statement. This cowl is meant to tuck snugly into the opening of your coat to give you just the right amount of color.

FINISHED MEASUREMENTS
Height: 12"/30.5 cm
Circumference: 24"/61 cm

YARN
Hometown USA by Lion Brand Yarn, super bulky #6 yarn
   (100% acrylic; 81 yds./74 m, 5 oz./142 g per skein)
1 skein #149 Dallas Grey (Color A)
1 skein #171 Key Lime (Color B)
1 skein #153 Oakland Black (Color C)

NEEDLES AND OTHER MATERIALS
- US 13 (10 mm) 24"/61 cm circular needle
- Stitch marker
- Yarn needle

GAUGE
9 sts x 12 rnds in St st = 4"/10 cm square

NOTES
- As you switch between colors, carry the nonworking yarns up the inside of the cowl by simply twisting one over the other. Be careful to maintain an even tension when you pick up a new color to avoid puckering. Cut the yarns when the cowl is finished.

Directions

With Color A, loosely cast on 54 stitches. Place stitch marker and join to work in
   the round, being careful not to twist the cast-on stitches.

Rnds 1–3: With Color A, knit.

Drop Color A. Join Color B.

Rnd 4: Knit.

Rnd 5: Purl.

Drop Color B. Join Color C.

Rnds 6–8: Knit.

Drop Color C. Join Color B.

Rnd 9: Knit.

Rnd 10: Purl.

Drop Color B.

Repeat Rnds 1–10 until piece measures 9"/23 cm from cast-on edge.

Work Rnds 1–3 once more.

Bind off loosely.

Weave in yarn ends.

Del Mar Derby Wrap

Make your knits and purls fall in line round after round to create a springy ribbed wrap. Knitted with alpaca yarn, this cowl is soft, light, and lofty, perfect for a day spent outside. You can wear it draped loosely around your shoulders or doubled up for extra warmth.

FINISHED MEASUREMENTS
Height: 16"/41 cm
Circumference: 32"/82 cm relaxed; stretches to 60"/152 cm

YARN
Baby Alpaca Grande by Plymouth Yarn, bulky weight #5 yarn
    (100% baby alpaca; 110 yds./100 m, 3.5 oz./100 g per skein)
3 skeins #8524 Aran

NEEDLES AND OTHER MATERIALS
- US 10$\frac{1}{2}$ (6.5 mm) 32"/82 cm circular needle
- Stitch marker
- Yarn needle

GAUGE
12 sts x 18 rnds in St st = 4"/10 cm square

NOTES
- This wrap is completely reversible so take care when weaving
  in the yarn ends!

Directions

Loosely cast on 148 stitches. Place marker and join to work in the round, being careful not to twist the cast-on stitches.

Rnd 1: *K2, p2; rep from * around.

Repeat Rnd 1 until piece measures 16"/41 cm from cast-on edge.

Bind off loosely in pattern.

Weave in yarn ends. Block cowl.

Date Night Infinity Loop

Dress up a simple outfit with a plush wrap in your favorite self-striping yarn. Wear it long as a loop (see page 14) or double it up for a cozy neck warmer (see page 12). There's an extra twist, two in fact, that make the loop captivating.

FINISHED MEASUREMENTS
Width: 8"/20 cm
Circumference: 55"/140 cm

YARN
Gina Chunky by Plymouth Yarn, chunky #5 yarn (100% wool; 131 yds./120 m, 3.5 oz./100 g per skein)
3 skeins #0101 Mermaid

NEEDLES AND OTHER MATERIALS
- US 11 (10 mm) 16"/41 cm circular needle
- Stitch marker
- Yarn needle

GAUGE
12 sts x 17 rnds in St st = 4"/10 cm square

NOTES
- Before you begin, match up the color changes at the beginning and end of the skeins to keep an even color flow.
- If you'd prefer to knit the ends of the scarf together rather than sew them as directed here, begin the project with a Provisional Cast-On. When you're finished, pull the waste yarn out, capture the live stitches, and graft the ends together using the Kitchener Stitch; see page 103 and 105 for photo tutorials on Provisional Cast-On and Kitchener.

Directions

Cast on 50 stitches, leaving a 1-yd./1-m tail. Place stitch marker and join to work in the round, being careful not to twist the cast-on stitches.

Rnd 1: Knit.

Repeat Rnd 1 until piece measures 55"/140 cm from cast-on edge or until desired length.

Bind off loosely.

Weave in interior yarn ends.

Lay scarf flat. Twist end of scarf two times. Sew cast-on edge to bind-off edge.

Weave in yarn ends. Block scarf.

Sea Glass Cowl

Sometimes you come across a yarn that is so special you've just got to knit something from it so you can admire it. Sea Glass Cowl is a simple design that lets this beautiful beaded yarn shine. Soft and lightweight, it's perfect when you want just a hint of warmth.

FINISHED MEASUREMENTS
Height: 12"/30.5 cm
Circumference: 24"/61 cm

YARN
Beaded Mohair by Artyarns, light worsted weight #3 yarn (60% silk, 40% kid mohair strung with glass beads; 170 yds./146 m, 1.75 oz./50 g per skein)
1 skein #921

NEEDLES AND OTHER MATERIALS
- US 8 (5 mm) 16"/41 cm circular needle
- Stitch marker
- Yarn needle

GAUGE
20 sts x 26 rnds in St st = 4"/10 cm square

Directions

Loosely cast on 106 stitches. Place marker and join to work in the round, being careful not to twist the cast-on stitches.

Rnd 1: Knit.

Repeat Rnd 1 until piece measures 12"/30.5 cm from cast-on edge or until desired length.

Bind off loosely.

Weave in yarn ends. Block cowl.

Adorned

This infinity scarf offers an eye-catching combination of function and style. Predominantly knit from a super bulky 100% wool yarn that will keep you toasty warm, it is embellished with a colorful band of sparkly wool-blend yarn that includes recycled sari silk. Adorned is sure to whisk away your winter blues!

FINISHED MEASUREMENTS
Width: 8"/20 cm
Circumference: 55"/140 cm

YARN
Sister Yarn by Knit Collage, super bulky weight #6 yarn (100% wool; 115 yds./105 m, 7.5 oz./215 g per skein)
2 skeins Camel Heather (Color A)
Rolling Stone by Knit Collage, super bulky weight #6 yarn (69% wool, 21% mohair, 9% recycled sari silk, 1% angelina sparkle; 40 yds./36.5 m, 4.5 oz./125 g per skein)
1 skein Boho Dance (Color B)

NEEDLES AND OTHER MATERIALS
• US 15 (10 mm) 16"/41 cm circular needle
• Stitch marker
• Yarn needle

GAUGE
8 sts x 12 rnds in St st = 4"/10 cm square in Color A.

Directions

With Color A, loosely cast on 40 sts, leaving a 1-yd./1-m tail. Place stitch marker
   and join to work in the round, being careful not to twist the cast-on stitches.

Rnd 1: Knit.

Repeat Rnd 1 until piece measures approximately 42"/107cm or until you are
   nearly out of Color A.

Join Color B.

Next rnd: Purl.

Continue purling all rnds until nearly out of Color B.

Bind off purlwise.

Using tail at cast-on edge, sew cast-on edge to bind-off edge.

Weave in yarn ends.

Basket Case Infinity Scarf

The basketweave stitch combines knits and purls in alternating blocks to give the illusion of a woven fabric. The Basket Case can be worn long or wrapped up to three times for a variety of different, creative looks to suit your style!

FINISHED MEASUREMENTS
Height: 9"/23 cm
Circumference: 72"/183 cm

YARN
Wooly Worsted by Ewe Ewe Yarns, medium worsted weight #4 yarn
(100% merino wool; 95 yds./87 m, 1.75 oz./50 g per skein)
4 skeins #10 Berry

NEEDLES AND OTHER MATERIALS
- US 10 (6 mm) 32"/81 cm circular needle
- Stitch marker
- Yarn needle

GAUGE
16 sts x 24 rnds in St st = 4"/10 cm square

NOTES
- This scarf is fully reversible, so take care when weaving in the yarn ends.

Directions

Loosely cast on 216 stitches. Place stitch marker and join to work in the round, being careful not to twist the cast-on stitches.

Rnds 1–18: *K12, p12; rep from * around.
Rnds 19–37: *P12, k12; rep from * around.
Rnds 38–56: *K12, p12; rep from * around.
Bind off loosely in pattern.
Weave in yarn ends. Block scarf.

Lovely Lace

Eyelets, loops, and dancing stitches make lace knitting fun and interesting. The combination of increases and decreases moves the patterns from round to round. Lace is lovely and adds a touch of elegance to any outfit. The light drape of a knitted silk lace scarf makes the perfect cover-up for a cool summer night at the beach. Use a yarn with a hint of sparkle to brighten up your basics. Each yarn selected in this chapter shows off the pattern stitches so your hard work isn't hidden away but shines like it should!

A Touch of Glitter Cowl

Pretty picot edges highlight a diamond lace pattern that is both enjoyable to knit and a pleasure to wear! It is knit with a silk yarn that consists of three different colors inspired by the fabrics and colors of India plied together with a strand of shiny silver Lurex® for just a touch of sparkle. A great one-skein project!

FINISHED MEASUREMENTS
Height: 8"/20.5 cm
Circumference: 40"/101.5 cm

YARN
Maharani Silk by Knit Collage, medium worsted weight #4 yarn (99% silk, 1% Lurex®; 185 yds./169 m, 3.5 oz./100 g per skein)
1 skein Bollywood Pink

NEEDLES AND OTHER MATERIALS
- US 6 (4 mm) 32"/81.5 cm circular needle
- Stitch marker
- Yarn needle

GAUGE
16 sts x 20 rnds in St st = 4"/10 cm square

SPECIAL STITCHES
Ssk
One at a time, slip the next 2 sts as if to knit. Insert LH needle into fronts of the 2 sts and knit together.
Picot Cast-On
Using a cable cast-on, cast on 5 sts. *Knit 2 sts, bind off 2 sts, cast on 4 sts; rep from * until required number of sts are on needle; for a photo tutorial, see page 95.
Picot Bind-Off
Using a cable cast-on, *cast on 2 sts, bind off 5 sts, slip last st back onto LH needle; rep from * until only 1 st is left on RH needle, and fasten off; for a photo tutorial, see page 96.

Directions

Using Picot Cast-On, cast on 160 stitches. Place a stitch marker and join to work in the round, being careful not to twist the cast-on stitches.

Rnd 1: Knit.

Rnd 2: *K1, k2tog, yo, k1, yo, ssk, k2; rep from * around.

Rnd 3: Knit.

Rnd 4: *K2tog, yo, k3, yo, ssk, k1; rep from * around.

Rnd 5: Knit.

Rnd 6: *Yo, k5, yo, sl 1 purlwise, k2tog, psso; rep from * around.

Rnd 7: Knit.

Rnd 8: *Yo, ssk, k3, k2tog, yo, k1; rep from * around.

Rnd 9: Knit.

Rnd 10: *K1, yo, ssk, k1, k2tog, yo, k2; rep from * around.

Rnd 11: Knit.

Rnd 12: *K2, yo, sl 1 purlwise, K2tog, psso, yo, k3; rep from * around.

Repeat Rnds 1–12 until piece measures 7$\frac{1}{2}$"/19 cm from cast-on edge.

Bind off using Picot Bind-off.

Weave in yarn ends and block scarf.

Save the Sunset Neck Warmer

As the day winds down, sometimes you need just a hint of warmth. Wrap Save the Sunset around you to brush off the chill while you watch the sun dip. This lace stitch works a bit differently since you don't need to place a stitch marker. With the right number of stitches, the pattern in the self-striping yarn used for this design creates striking angled stripes.

FINISHED MEASUREMENTS
Height: 9"/23 cm
Circumference: 25"/63.5 cm

YARN
Crazy Zauberball by Schoppel-Wolle, super fine
    weight #1 yarn (75% superwash wool, 25% nylon;
    459 yds./419 m, 3.5 oz./100 g per skein)
1 skein #2170

NEEDLES AND OTHER MATERIALS
• US 4 (3.5 mm) 16"/41 cm circular needle
• Stitch marker
• Yarn needle

GAUGE
26 sts x 34 rnds in St st = 4"/10 cm

Directions

Loosely cast on 156 stitches. Do not place marker! Join to work in the round, being careful not to twist the cast-on stitches.

*K6, ssk, k2tog, yo, k1, yo; rep from * in continuous rnds until piece measures approximately 4"/10 cm from cast-on edge.

Knit all rnds until piece measures 9"/23 cm from cast-on edge.

Bind off loosely.

Weave in yarn ends. Block cowl.

Beach Break Loop

This linen scarf is perfect for a breezy summer's evening. The center lace stitch features long, undulating stitches that move like the calm seas. The border lace pattern has a unique elongated loop that, with its repetition, reminds me of breaking waves. Meet the Beach Break Loop!

FINISHED MEASUREMENTS
Width: 8"/20 cm
Circumference: 55"/140 cm

YARN
Linen Concerto by Plymouth Yarn, medium worsted weight #4 yarn
  (48% rayon, 42% linen, 10% cotton; 101 yds./92 m, 1.75 oz./50 g
  per skein)
5 skeins #06 Chambray

NEEDLES AND OTHER MATERIALS
• US 7 (4.5 mm) 32"/81 cm circular needle
• Stitch marker
• Yarn needle

GAUGE
16 sts x 24 rnds in St st = 4"/10 cm square

Directions

Loosely cast on 224 stitches. Place stitch marker and join to work in the round, being careful not to twist the cast-on stitches.

First Slip Stitch Lace Section

Rnd 1: Knit.
Rnd 2: *Yo, k4; rep from * around.
Rnd 3: *Drop yo from previous rnd, yo, sl 1 knitwise, k3, psso; rep from * around.
Rnd 4: Knit.
Repeat Rnds 1–4 until piece measures 4"/10 cm from cast-on edge.

Stockinette Stretch Section

Rnds 1–6: Knit.
Rnd 7: *K1, yo; rep from * around.
Rnd 8: *K1, drop yo from previous rnd; rep from * around.
Repeat Rnds 1–8 until piece measures 10"/25.5 cm from cast-on edge.
Work Rnds 1–6 once more.

Second Slip Stitch Lace Section

Work Rnds 1–4 of First Slip Stitch Lace Section until piece measures 15"/38 cm from cast-on edge.

Bind Off

Bind off loosely.
Weave in yarn ends. Block cowl.

Changing Tides Cowl

The lace pattern for Changing Tides looks challenging but it's not! The waves of eyelets simply move over one position on each round. Probably the hardest thing about this pattern will be casting on 300 stitches!

FINISHED MEASUREMENTS
Height: 12"/30.5 cm
Circumference: 40"/101.5 cm

YARN
Peppino by The Yarns of Rhichard Devrieze, super fine weight #1 yarn (100% merino wool; 225 yds./206 m, 2.5 oz./65 g per skein)
2 skeins Frankly Scarlet

NEEDLES AND OTHER MATERIALS
- US 5 (3.75 mm) 32"/81 cm circular needle
- Stitch marker
- Yarn needle

GAUGE
26 sts x 32 rnds in St st = 4"/10 cm square

Directions

Loosely cast on 300 stitches. Place stitch marker and join to work in the round, being careful not to twist the cast-on stitches.

Rnd 1: *K4, k2tog, yo; rep from * around.
Rnd 2: *K3, k2tog, k1, yo; rep from * around.
Rnd 3: *K2, k2tog, k2, yo; rep from * around.
Rnd 4: *K1, k2tog, k3, yo; rep from * around.
Rnd 5: *K2tog, k4, yo; rep from * around.

Rnd 6: Remove marker, sl 1, place marker, *yo, k4, k2tog; rep from * around.
Rnd 7: *K1, yo, k3, k2tog; rep from * around.
Rnd 8: *K2, yo, k2, k2tog; rep from * around.
Rnd 9: *K3, yo, k1, k2tog; rep from * around.
Rnd 10: *K4, yo, k2tog; rep from * around.

Repeat Rnds 1–10 until piece measures 5"/13 cm from the cast-on edge.

Bind off loosely knitwise.

Weave in yarn ends. Block cowl.

Seaside Lace Capelet

This lightweight shoulder wrap is the perfect protection from gentle summer breezes. The nested lace stitch develops columns of decorative eyelets and pretty fans. The silk in this yarn blend gives the capelet a relaxed drape, while the inclusion of cashmere provides softness and warmth.

FINISHED MEASUREMENTS
Length: 16"/40.5 cm
Circumference: 40"/101.5 cm

YARN
Ensemble Light by Artyarns, sport weight #2 yarn (50% silk, 50% cashmere; 400 yds./366 m, 3 oz./80 g per skein)
1 skein #2241

NEEDLES AND OTHER MATERIALS
- US 8 (5 mm) 24"/61 cm circular needle
- US 10^1/$_2$ (6.5 mm) 24"/61 cm circular needle
- Stitch marker
- Yarn needle

GAUGE
16 sts x 20 rnds in St st on larger needles = 4"/10 cm square

NOTES
- To narrow the neckline of the capelet, you will change to a smaller needle rather than decreasing the number of stitches.

SPECIAL STITCHES
Skp
Slip 1 st knitwise, knit the next st, insert LH needle through front loop of slipped st, and pass it over the knit st—1 st dec'd.

Directions

With larger needle, cast on 162 stitches. Place stitch marker and join to work in
the round, being careful not to twist the cast-on stitches.

Rnd 1: *K1, yo, k2, skp, k2tog, k2, yo; rep from * around.

Rnd 2: Knit.

Rnd 3: *Yo, k2, skp, k2tog, k2, yo, k1; rep from * around.

Rnd 4: Knit.

Repeat Rnds 1–4 until piece measures 12"/30.5 cm from cast-on edge.

Next rnd: Knit.

Repeat last rnd until piece measures 14"/35.5 cm from cast-on edge.

Change to smaller needle and continue to knit each rnd until piece measures
16"/40.5 cm from cast-on edge.

Bind off.

Weave in yarn ends. Block cowl. If desired, to highlight the eyelets and scalloped
edge, pin each point when blocking.

Cables, Twists & Bobbles

Changing between knits and purls at the right time can add depth and texture to your finished piece. Make a scarf with a twist, add a cable to your cowl, knit a billion bobbles! You'll find all of these techniques and more on the scarves in this chapter. Take your texture up a notch!

High Speed Cable Cowl

Big needles and a basic cable stitch make for a fast project! Traditional cable needles may be too small to hold this super bulky yarn, so reach for a double-pointed needle if that's the case. Choose a hand-dyed yarn with subtle color variation to add extra visual interest.

FINISHED MEASUREMENTS
Width: 11"/28 cm
Circumference: 48"/122

YARN
Franca by Manos del Uruguay, super bulky weight #6 yarn (100% superwash merino wool; 114 yds./104 m, 5.25 oz./150 g per skein)
2 skeins #F20 Granada

NEEDLES AND OTHER MATERIALS
- US 13 (9 mm) 32"/81 cm circular needle
- Stitch marker
- Cable needle
- Yarn needle

GAUGE
10 sts x 18 rnds in St st = 4"/10 cm square

SPECIAL STITCHES
C8F
Slip 4 sts to cable needle, hold to front, knit 4 sts from LH needle, knit 4 sts from cable needle.

Directions

Loosely cast on 120 stitches. Place stitch marker and join to work in the round, being careful not to twist the cast-on stitches.

Rnds 1–7: *K8, p7; rep from * around.

Rnd 8: *C8F, p7; rep from * around.

Repeat Rnds 1–8 until piece measures 9"/23 cm from cast-on edge.

Next 4 rnds: *K8, p7; rep from * around.

Bind off in pattern.

Weave in yarn ends. Block cowl.

Sweater Weather Scarf

Cables and twists come together to work like your favorite casual sweater. This is a long, cozy, double-thick tube scarf sure to keep you warm no matter how cold it is outside!

FINISHED MEASUREMENTS
Length: 72"/183 cm
Width: 10"/25.5 cm

YARN
Zara Melange by Filatura Di Crosa, light worsted weight #3 yarn (100% merino wool; 136 yds./124 m, 1.75 oz./50 g per skein)
8 skeins #1481 Denim Heather

NEEDLES AND OTHER MATERIALS
- US 7 (4.5 mm) 16"/41 cm circular needle
- Stitch marker
- Cable needle
- Yarn needle

GAUGE
20 sts x 24 rnds in St st = 4"/10 cm

NOTES
- The ends of the scarf are left open like a sleeve.

SPECIAL STITCHES
RC (Right Cross)
Knit into second st on LH needle, knit into first st on LH needle, slip both sts to RH needle.

C4F
Slip 2 sts to cable needle, hold to the front, knit 2 sts from LH needle, knit 2 sts from cable needle.

C6F
Slip 3 sts to cable needle, hold to the front, knit 3 sts from LH needle, knit 3 sts from cable needle.

Directions

Cast on 84 stitches. Place stitch marker and join to work in the round, being careful not to twist the cast-on stitches.

Ribbing rnd: *K2, p2; rep from * around.

Work Ribbing rnd until piece measures 6"/15 cm from cast-on edge.

Rnds 1–4: *P4, k4, p2, k2, p2, k4, p4, k6; rep from * around.

Rnd 5: *P4, k4, p2, RC, p2, k4, p4, k6; rep from * around.

Rnd 6: Rep Rnd 1.

Rnd 7: *P4, k4, p2, RC, p2, k4, p4, C6F; rep from * around.

Rnd 8: Rep Rnd 1.

Rnd 9: Rep Rnd 5.

Rnds 10–14: Rep Rnd 1.

Rnd 15: * P4, C4F, p2, k2, p2, C4F, p4, k6; rep from * around.

Rnd 16: Rep Rnd 1.

Repeat Rnds 1–16 until piece measures 66"/168 cm from cast-on edge.

Work Ribbing rnd until scarf measures 72"/183 cm from cast-on edge.

Bind off in pattern.

Weave in yarn ends. Block scarf.

Tangerine Twist

Take your taste buds on a trip with the Tangerine Twist. The cables in this pattern move the stitches outward like branches from a tree. Pick a brightly colored yarn and watch this cowl grow in just an evening or two!

FINISHED MEASUREMENTS
Height: 12"/30.5 cm
Circumference: 24"/61 cm

YARN
Wool-Ease Thick & Quick by Lion Brand Yarns, super bulky weight #6 yarn (80% acrylic, 20% wool; 106 yds./97 m, 6 oz./170 g per skein)
2 skeins #133 Pumpkin

NEEDLES AND OTHER MATERIALS
- US 13 (9 mm) 24"/61 cm circular needle
- Stitch marker
- Cable needle
- Yarn needle

GAUGE
8 sts x 15 rnds in St st = 4"/10 cm square

SPECIAL STITCHES
C4B
Slip 2 sts to cable needle, hold to the back, knit 2 sts from LH needle, knit 2 sts from cable needle.
C4F
Work as for C4B but hold cable needle to the front.

Directions

Loosely cast on 72 stitches. Place stitch marker and join to work in the round, being careful not to twist the cast-on stitches.

Rnd 1: Knit.

Rnd 2: Purl.

Rnds 3–4: Rep Rnds 1–2.

Rnds 5, 7, and 9: *P1, k16, p1; rep from * around.

Rnd 6: *P1, k4, C4B, C4F, k4, p1; rep from * around.

Rnd 8: *P1, k2, C4B, k4, C4F, k2, p1; rep from * around.

Rnd 10: *P1, C4B, k8, C4F, p1; rep from * around.

Repeat Rnds 5–10 a total of 4 times.

Rep Rnds 5–7.

Next rnd: Purl.

Next rnd: Knit.

Next rnd: Purl.

Next rnd: Knit.

Bind off loosely.

Weave in all yarn ends.

Double Agent Wrap

The Double Agent can be worn as either a big, drapey cowl or as a belted shrug (see page 56) to keep the chill from your shoulders. But don't reveal all your secrets—this is a mock cable posing as the real thing!

FINISHED MEASUREMENTS
Width: 15"/38 cm
Circumference: 60"/152.5 cm

YARN
Wooly Worsted by Ewe Ewe Yarns, medium worsted weight #4 yarn
    (100% merino wool; 95 yds./87 m, 1.75 oz./50 g per skein)
8 skeins #91 Wheat

NEEDLES AND OTHER MATERIALS
- US 9 (5.5 mm) 32"/81 cm circular needle
- Stitch marker
- Yarn needle

GAUGE
16 sts x 24 rnds in St st = 4"/10 cm square

SPECIAL STITCHES
Skp
Slip 1 st knitwise, knit next st, insert LH needle through front loop of
    slipped st, and pass it over the knit st—1 st dec'd.

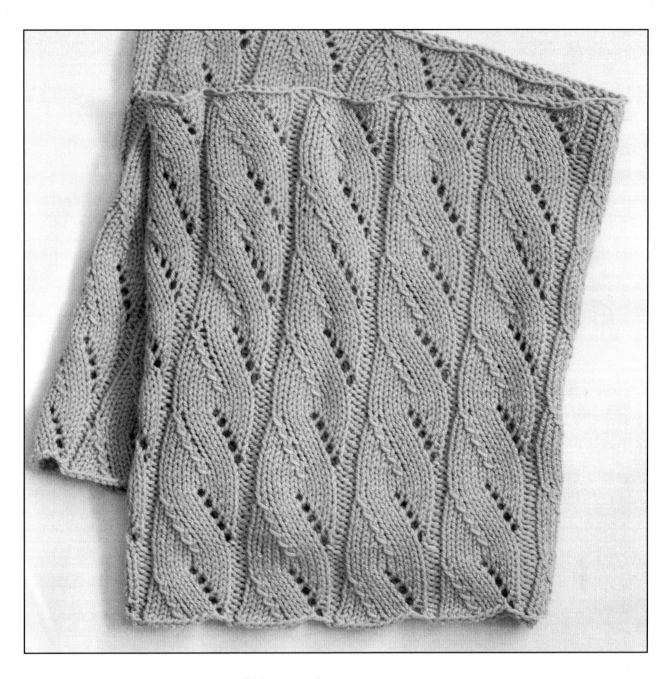

Directions

Loosely cast on 231 stitches. Place stitch marker and join to work in the round, being careful not to twist the cast-on stitches.

Rnd 1: *P2, yo, k3, skp, k4; rep from * around.

Rnd 2 and all even-numbered rnds: *P2, k9; rep from * around.

Rnd 3: *P2, k1, yo, k3, skp, k3; rep from * around.

Rnd 5: *P2, k2, yo, k3, skp, k2; rep from * around.

Rnd 7: *P2, k3, yo, k3, skp, k1; rep from * around.

Rnd 9: *P2, k4, yo, k3, skp; rep from * around.

Rnds 11–12: Rep Rnd 2.

Work Rnds 1–12 for a total of 6 times.

Rep Rnds 1–9 one more time.

Bind off in pattern as for Rnd 10, *P2, k9 rep from * around.

Weave in yarn ends. Block scarf.

Popcorn & Purls

Wrap yourself in lots of soft bobbles with this infinity scarf. Sections of garter stitch, stockinette stitch, and bobbles alternate around the scarf and show off their unique textures when wrapped. This generous scarf will easily wrap three times.

FINISHED MEASUREMENTS
Width: 6"/15 cm
Circumference: 60"/152.5 cm

YARN
Wooly Worsted by Ewe Ewe Yarns, medium worsted weight #4 yarn
   (100% merino wool; 95 yds./87 m, 1.75 oz./50 g per skein)
6 skeins #50 Pistachio

NEEDLES AND OTHER MATERIALS
• US 8 (5 mm) 32"/81 cm circular needle
• Stitch marker
• Yarn needle

GAUGE
18 sts x 24 rnds in St st = 4"/10 cm square

SPECIAL STITCHES
MB (make bobble)
Make 5 stitches in 1 stitch as follows: Knit in the front, back, front, back, and front of the same stitch. TURN. Purl 5. TURN. Knit 5. TURN. Purl 5. TURN. K2tog, k2tog, knit 1, slip the first 2 stitches over the last stitch and off the needle, leaving one stitch.

Directions

Loosely cast on 276 stitches. Place stitch marker and join to work in the round, being careful not to twist the cast-on stitches.

Rnd 1 and all odd-numbered rnds: Knit.

Rnd 2: *P25, k1, [MB, k5] 3 times, MB, k27, [MB, k5] 3 times, MB, k1; rep from * around.

Rnd 3: Knit.

Rnd 4: *P25, k67; rep from * around.

Rnd 5: Knit.

Rnd 6: *P25, k4 [MB, k5] 2 times, MB, k33, [MB, k5] 2 times, MB, k4; rep from * around.

Rnd 7: Knit.

Rnd 8: *P25, k67; rep from * around.

Repeat Rnds 1–8 until piece measures 6"/15 cm from cast-on edge.

Bind off loosely in pattern.

Weave in yarn ends. Block scarf.

Entrelac Effect Neck Warmer

Entrelac knitting is fun and surprisingly straightforward. While you'll have lots of stitches on your needle, you'll only be working a few at any given moment. You'll flip this work back and forth, unlike any other scarf in this book, but simply work each section as described and build the Entrelac Effect one brick at a time!

FINISHED MEASUREMENTS
Height: 8"/20.5 cm
Circumference: 24"/61 cm

YARN
Effektgarn by Kauni, sport weight #2 yarn (100% wool; 616 yds./563 m, 5 oz./140 g per skein)
1 skein EPA

NEEDLES AND OTHER MATERIALS
- US 6 (4 mm) 16"/41 cm circular needle
- Stitch marker
- Yarn needle

GAUGE
24 sts x 32 rnds in St st = 4"/10 cm square

NOTES
- To get the stripes you see here, choose a self-striping yarn with long color transitions.

SPECIAL STITCHES
Ssk
One at a time, slip next 2 sts as if to knit. Insert LH needle into fronts of the 2 sts and knit together—1 st dec'd.

Directions

Cast on 80 stitches. Place stitch marker and join to work in the round, being careful not to twist the cast-on stitches.

Base Triangles

*Row 1 (RS): K1, turn.
Row 2 (WS): P1, turn.
Row 3: K2, turn.
Row 4: P2, turn.
Row 5: K3, turn.
Row 6: P3, turn.
Row 7: K4, turn.
Row 8: P4, turn.
Row 9: K5, turn.
Row 10: P5, turn.
Row 11: K6, turn.
Row 12: P6, turn.
Row 13: K7, turn.
Row 14: P7, turn.
Row 15: K8. Do not turn.
Repeat from * 9 times more—10 Base Triangles made.
Turn work to WS.

Wrong Side Rectangles

****With WS facing, pick up and purl 8 sts down left edge of first Base Triangle. Turn.
Next row (RS): K8, turn.
*Next row (WS): P7, p2tog (the last st of current rectangle and the first st of Base Triangle), turn.
Next row: K8, turn.
Rep from * until all sts from first Base Triangle are worked.
Next row: P7, p2tog (8 sts on RH needle). Do not turn.**
Repeat from ** to ** to work all 10 Rectangles.
Turn work to RS.

Right Side Rectangles

**With RS facing, with RH needle pick up and knit 8 sts
down left side of first WS Rectangle. Turn.
*Next row (WS):** P8, turn.
Next row (RS): K7, ssk (first st from RS of rectangle and first
st from WS rectangle), turn.*
Repeat from * to * until all sts from WS Rectangle are
worked. Do not turn.**
Repeat from ** to ** until 10 RS Rectangles have been
made.
On the very last RS row, turn work to WS.

Finish Rectangles

Repeat Wrong Side Rectangles and Right Side Rectangles
sections 2 more times.

End Triangles

*With WS facing, with RH needle, pick up and knit 8 sts
down side of first RS Rectangle. Turn.
Row 1 (RS): K8, turn.
Row 2: P2tog, p5, p2tog (last st of End Triangle and first st
of RS Rectangle), turn.
Row 3: K7, turn.
Row 4: P2tog, p4, p2tog, turn.
Row 5: K6, turn.
Row 6: P2tog, p3, p2tog, turn.
Row 7: K5, turn.
Row 8: P2tog, p2, p2tog, turn.
Row 9: K4, turn.
Row 10: P2tog, p1, p2tog, turn.
Row 11: K3, turn.
Row 12: P2tog, p2tog, turn.
Row 13: K2, turn.
Row 14: P2tog, p2tog, pass 1st over 2nd st—1 st remains
on RH needle. Do not turn.*
Repeat from * to * 9 times more but only pick up 7 sts, since
you will already have 1 st from previous End Triangle
already on needle.
Fasten off and weave in yarn ends. Block scarf.

Cozy Colorwork

Make bold, graphic patterns, knit one-row stripes, use lots of colors in the same project! Knitting in the round allows adventurous forms of colorful knitting. Many of the patterns use a technique called stranded knitting and while they may employ lots of colors, you'll only ever be alternating between two yarns at one time. Follow the charts and you're on your way!

Pixel Perfect

Little boxes of color-changing yarn add just the right amount of playfulness to this simple tube scarf. If you are new to stranded knitting, this simple Fair Isle design will help you develop an even tension and technique.

FINISHED MEASUREMENTS
Width: 8"/20.5 cm
Length: 70"/178 cm

YARN
Ewe So Sporty by Ewe Ewe Yarns, sport weight #2 yarn (100% merino wool; 145 yds./132.5 m, 1.75 oz./50 g per skein)
5 skeins #97 Brushed Silver (Color A)
Ombré Sport by Freia Fibers, sport weight #2 yarn (100% wool; 217 yds./198.5 m, 2.75 oz./75 g skein)
1 skein Melon (Color B)

NEEDLES AND OTHER MATERIALS
- US 5 (3.5 mm) 16"/41 cm circular needle
- Stitch marker
- Yarn needle

GAUGE
22 sts x 26 rnds in St st = 4"/10 cm square

NOTES
- When working with two colors, carry the nonworking color with an even tension behind the working color. Change between the two strands in a consistent manner, such as Color A over and Color B under, and the yarns will remain untangled and you will avoid gaps in the work.
- The ends of this scarf remain open and will curl slightly.

Directions

With Color A, cast on 88 stitches. Place stitch marker and join to work in the round, being careful not to twist the cast-on stitches.

Rnds 1–2: With Color A, knit.

Rnds 3–4: *K2 with Color A, k2 with Color B; rep from * around.

Work Rnds 1–4 until piece measures 70"/178 cm from cast-on edge.

Work Rnds 1–2 one time more.

Cut Color B. Bind off with Color A.

Weave in yarn ends. Block scarf.

Desert Dreams

Take a trip to the Southwest with this graphic print cowl. Desert Dreams is worked in a tube and the ends are grafted together to form a cozy loop.

FINISHED MEASUREMENTS
Width: 8"/20.5 cm
Circumference: 24"/61 cm

YARN
Suri Merino by Blue Sky Alpacas, light worsted weight #3 yarn (60% baby suri alpaca, 40% merino; 164 yds./149 m, 3.5 oz./100 g per skein)
2 skeins # 415 Harvest (Color A)
1 skein # 418 Dusk (Color B)

NEEDLES AND OTHER MATERIALS
- 2 US 7 (4.5 mm) 16"/41 cm circular needles
- US K-9 (5.5 mm) crochet hook
- 2-yd./2-m length of smooth scrap yarn in a contrasting color from main color
- Stitch marker
- Yarn needle

GAUGE
20 sts x 24 rnds in St st = 4"/10 cm square

NOTES
- When following the color chart, carry the nonworking color with an even tension behind the working color. Change between the two strands in a consistent manner, such as Color A over and Color B under, and the yarns will remain untangled and you will avoid gaps in the work. For longer color change sections in this cowl, twist the strands to capture the nonworking color. See page 102 for a photo tutorial.
- For photo tutorials for Provisional Cast-On and Kitchener Stitch, see pages 103 and 105.

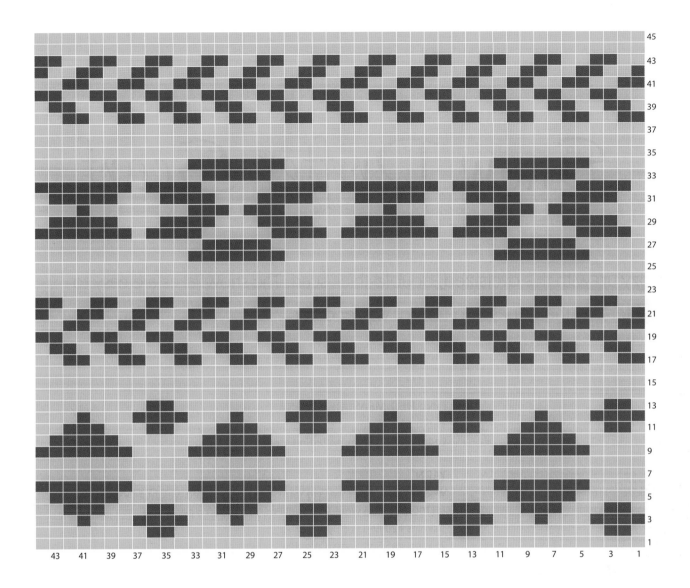

Directions

With Color A and using a Provisional Cast-On, cast on 88 stitches. Place stitch marker and join to work in the round, being careful not to twist the cast-on stitches.

Rnd 1: Knit.

Rnd 2: Knit Rnd 1 of Desert Dreams patt chart, repeating patt 2 times around.

Continue to work as established through all 45 rnds of Desert Dreams patt chart for a total of 3 times.

Do not bind off.

Carefully weave in all internal yarn ends.

Gently remove waste yarn from Provisional Cast-On, transfer live sts to a needle, and graft to working end using Kitchener Stitch.

Weave in yarn end. Block cowl.

Snow Drifter Scarf

Cozy up with this oversized, double-thick scarf. The snowflakes are easy to master and the stripes add tons of winter color.

FINISHED MEASUREMENTS
Width: 8"/20.5 cm
Length: 70"/178 cm, excluding fringe

YARN
Wooly Worsted by Ewe Ewe Yarns, medium worsted weight #4 yarn
   (100% merino wool; 95 yds./87 m, 1.75 oz./50 g per skein)
3 skeins #20 Red Poppy (Color A)
2 skeins #45 Soft Sage (Color B)
4 skeins #90 Vanilla (Color C)
2 skeins #05 Cotton Candy (Color D)
2 skeins #70 Aquamarine (Color E)

NEEDLES AND OTHER MATERIALS
- US 7 (4.5 mm) 32"/81 cm circular needle
- Stitch marker
- Yarn needle

GAUGE
20 sts x 24 rnds in St st = 4"/10 cm square

NOTES
- When following the color chart, carry the nonworking color with an even tension behind the working color. Change between the two strands in a consistent manner, such as Color A over and Color B under, and the yarns will remain untangled and you will avoid gaps in the work. See page 102 for a photo tutorial.
- The ends of this scarf are closed with the application of fringe.

Directions

With Color A, cast on 80 stitches. Place a stitch marker and join to work in the round, being careful not to twist the cast-on stitches.

Rnd 1: Knit.

Drop Color A. Join Color B.

Rnds 2–7: Knit.

Drop Color B.

Rnds 8–25: With Colors C and A, work Snowflake chart.

Drop Colors C and A. Join Color D.

Rnds 26–31: Knit.

Drop Color D. Join Color E.

Rnds 32–49: Knit.

Drop Color E.

Rnds 50–67: With Color C, knit.

Drop Color C.

Rnds 68–85: With Color A, knit.

Drop Color A.

Rnds 86–103: With Color C, knit.

Drop Color C.

Rnds 104–121: With Color B, knit.

Drop Color B.

Rnds 122–139: With Color C, knit.

Drop Color C.

Rnds 140–157: With Color D, knit.

Drop Color D.

Rnds 158–174: With Colors C and E, work Snowflake chart.

Drop Colors C and E.

Rnds 175–180: With Color A, knit.

Drop Color A.

Rnds 181–186: With Color D, knit.

Drop Color D.

Rnds 187–192: With Color A, knit.

Drop Color A.

Rnds 193–198: With Color D, knit.

Drop Color D.

Rnds 199–204: With Color A, knit.

Drop Color A.

Rnds 205–210: With Color B, knit.

Drop Color B.

Rnds 211–216: With Color A, knit.

Drop Color A.

Rnds 217–222: With Color B, knit.

Drop Color B.

Rnds 223–228: With Color A, knit.

Drop Color A.

Rnds 229–245: With Colors C and E, work Snowflake chart.

Drop C and E.

Rnds 246–263: With Color B, knit.

Drop Color B.

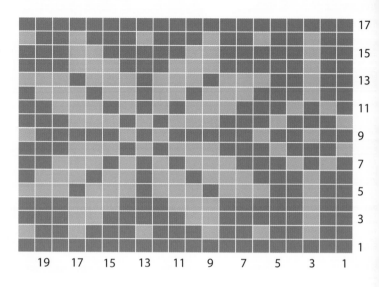

Rnds 264–281: With Color C, knit.

Drop Color C.

Rnds 282–299: With Color D, knit.

Drop Color D.

Rnds 300–317: With Color C, knit.

Drop Color C.

Rnds 318–335: With Color A, knit.

Drop Color A.

Rnds 336–353: With Color C, knit.

Drop Color C.

Rnds 354–371: With Color E, knit.

Drop Color E.

Rnds 372–377: With Color D, knit.

Drop Color D.

Rnds 378–394: With Colors C and A, work Snowflake chart.

Drop Colors C and A.

Rnds 395–400: With Color B, knit.

Drop Color B.

Rnds 401–402: With Color A, knit.

Bind off with Color A.

Fasten off all colors and weave in yarn ends. Block scarf and let dry completely.

Cut 64 (16"/41 cm) lengths of Color A for fringe. Lay scarf flat. Starting with the cast-on edge, insert crochet hook through both layers of the scarf end at one edge. Hold two lengths of fringe together and place on crochet hook. Pull fringe partly through scarf fabric to form a loop, pull ends through loop, and tug gently to secure, closing the end of the scarf. Repeat with two more fringe pieces at opposite edge of scarf. Add remaining fringe in the same manner, spacing evenly across the scarf for a total of 16 sets of fringe. Repeat for the opposite end of the scarf.

Blue Lagoon Infinity Scarf

The Blue Lagoon Infinity Scarf is long and can wrap two or even three times. While it looks like there is a lot of colorwork happening, it's really just stripes and slipped stitches. The large eyelets are easy to work and add a playfulness to this warm wrap.

FINISHED MEASUREMENTS
Width: 8"/20.5 cm
Circumference: 55"/140 cm

YARN
Extra by Blue Sky Alpacas, medium worsted weight #4 yarn (55% baby alpaca, 45% merino wool; 218 yds./199.5 m, 5.5 oz./150 g per skein)
1 skein #3518 Java (Color A)
1 skein #3516 Stillwater (Color B)

NEEDLES AND OTHER MATERIALS
- US 8 (4.5 mm) 32"/81.5 cm circular needle
- Stitch marker
- Yarn needle

GAUGE
20 sts x 24 rnds in St st = 4"/10 cm

NOTES
- Carry the nonworking yarn up the inside of the cowl, being sure not to pull too tightly to avoid puckering.
- For a photo tutorial for double yo, see page 101.

SPECIAL STITCHES
Skp
Slip 1 st knitwise, knit next st, insert LH needle through front loop of slipped st, and pass it over the knit st—1 st dec'd.

Directions

With Color A, loosely cast on 232 stitches. Place stitch marker and join to work in the round, being careful not to twist the cast-on stitches.

Rnd 1: Knit.

Rnd 2: Purl.

Drop Color A, join Color B.

Rnds 3–4: K1, *sl 2 wyib, k6*; rep from * to * around to last 7 sts, sl 2 wyib, k5.

Rnd 5: K1, *sl 2 wyib, k1, skp, yo 2 times, k2tog, k1*; rep from * to * around to last 7 sts, sl 2 wyib, k1, skp, yo 2 times, k2tog.

Rnd 6: K1, *sl 2 wyib, k2, [k1, p1] into double yo, k2*; rep from * to * around to last 7 sts, sl 2 wyib, k2, [k1, p1] into double yo, k1.

Rnd 7: Rep Rnd 3.

Drop Color B, join Color A.

Rnd 8: Knit.

Rnd 9: Purl.

Rnds 10–11: Rep Rnds 8–9.

Drop Color A, join Color B.

Rnds 12–13: K5, *sl 2 wyib, k6*; rep from * to * around to last 3 sts, k1, sl 2 wyib.

Rnd 14: K5, *sl 2 wyib, k1, skp, yo 2 times, k2tog, k1*; rep from * to * around to last 3 sts, k1, sl 2 wyib.

Rnd 15: K5, *sl 2 wyib, k2, [k1, p1] into double yo, k2*; rep from * to * around to last 3 sts, k1, sl 2 wyib.

Rnd 16: Rep Rnd 14.

Drop Color B, join Color A.

Rnd 17: Knit.

Rnd 18: Purl.

Rep Rnds 1–18 until piece measures 8"/20.5 cm, ending with a rnd working Color A.

Bind off loosely.

Weave in yarn ends. Block cowl.

The Harlequins

The diamond shapes in The Harlequins cowl make a classic design modern. Choose five colors that you wear often and this cowl will go with everything! The handspun nature of this yarn adds a funky irregularity to these otherwise perfect squares.

FINISHED MEASUREMENTS
Height: 12"/30.5 cm
Circumference: 32"/81 cm

YARN
Wool Clasica by Manos del Uruguay, medium worsted weight #4
    yarn (100% wool; 138 yds./126 m, 3.5 oz./100 g per skein)
1 skein #11 Navy (Color A)
1 skein #84 Mandarin (Color B)
1 skein #82 Shocking (Color C)
1 skein #S Magenta (Color D)
1 skein #05 Aqua (Color E)

NEEDLES AND OTHER MATERIALS
- US 9 (5.5 mm) 24"/61 cm circular needle
- Stitch marker
- Yarn needle

GAUGE
16 sts x 24 rnds in St st = 4"/10 cm

NOTES
- When following the color chart, carry the nonworking color with an even tension behind the working color. Change between the two strands in a consistent manner, such as Color A over and Color B under, and the yarns will remain untangled and you will avoid gaps in the work. See page 102 for a photo tutorial.
- The Harlequin pattern is a 6-stitch repeat.

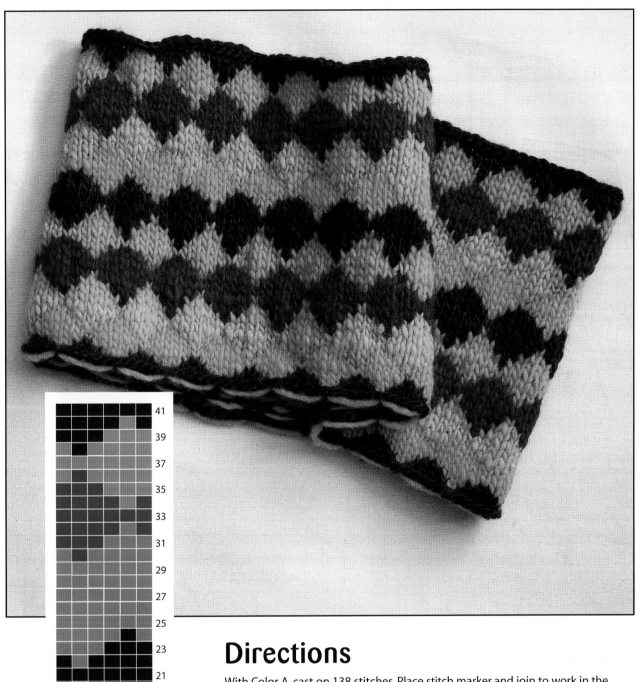

Directions

With Color A, cast on 138 stitches. Place stitch marker and join to work in the
    round, being careful not to twist the cast-on stitches.

Rnd 1: Knit.

Rnd 2: Knit Rnd 1 of Harlequin patt chart, repeating the patt 23 times around.

Continue to work as established through all 41 rnds of Harlequin patt chart
    one time.

Bind off loosely with Color A.

Weave in yarn ends. Block cowl.

Pretty Preppy

Get your preppy on with this argyle neck warmer. Worked up in two colors, it's easy to follow.

FINISHED MEASUREMENTS
Height: 9"/23 cm
Circumference: 20"/51 cm

YARN
Ewe So Sporty by Ewe Ewe Yarns, sport weight #2 yarn (100% merino
    wool; 145 yds./133 m, 1.75 oz./50 g per skein)
1 skein # 98 Charcoal (Color A)
1 skein # 05 Cotton Candy (Color B)

NEEDLES AND OTHER MATERIALS
- US 6 (4 mm) 16"/41 cm circular needle
- Stitch marker
- Yarn needle

GAUGE
22 sts x 26 rnds in St st = 4"/10 cm square

NOTES
- When following the color chart, carry the nonworking color with
  an even tension behind the working color. Change between the
  two strands in a consistent manner, such as Color A over and Color
  B under, and the yarns will remain untangled and you will avoid
  gaps in the work. For a photo tutorial on stranded knitting, see
  page 102.
- The Argyle pattern is a 12-stitch repeat.

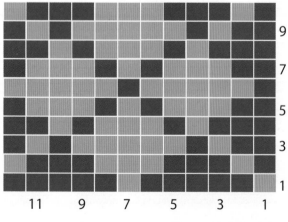

Directions

With Color A, cast on 120 stitches. Place stitch marker and
  join to work in the round, being careful not to twist the
  cast-on stitches.

Rnds 1–5: Purl.

Rnd 6: Knit.

Rnd 7: Knit Rnd 1 of Argyle patt chart, repeating patt 10
  times around.

Continue to work as established through all 10 rnds of
  Argyle patt chart, repeating chart until piece measures
  approximately 8"/20.5 cm from cast-on edge.

Next rnd: Knit Rnd 1 of Argyle patt chart.

Next rnd: With Color A, knit.

Next 5 rnds: Purl.

Bind off purlwise.

Weave in yarn ends. Block cowl.

Color Block Scarf

Basic black and white are worked together to create a mesmerizing pattern that can only be achieved by knitting in the round. Add two long blocks of your favorite colors and this scarf will be a staple in your winter wardrobe.

FINISHED MEASUREMENTS
Width: 8"/20.5 cm
Length: 72"/183 cm

YARN
Wooly Worsted by Ewe Ewe Yarns, medium worsted #4 yarn (100% merino wool; 95 yds./87 m, 1.75 oz./50 g per skein)
2 skeins #10 Berry (Color A)
2 skeins # 50 Pistachio (Color B)
2 skeins # 90 Vanilla (Color C)
2 skeins # 99 Black Licorice (Color D)

NEEDLES AND OTHER MATERIALS
- US 10^1/2 (6.5 mm) 16"/41 cm circular needle
- Stitch marker
- Yarn needle

GAUGE
16 sts x 16 rnds in St st = 4"/10 cm square

NOTES
- As you switch between colors, carry the nonworking yarns up the inside of the cowl by simply twisting one over the other. Be careful to maintain an even tension when you pick up a new color to avoid puckering. You will only need to cut the yarns when the striped section is finished.
- The ends of this scarf are left open and will curl slightly.

Directions

Color Block Section

With Color A, cast on 64 sts. Place stitch marker and join to work in the round, being careful not to twist the cast-on stitches.

Rnds 1–87: Knit.

Break Color A. Join Color B.

Rep Rnds 1–87.

Break Color B.

Striped Section

Rnd 1: With Color C, knit.

Drop Color C.

Rnd 2: With Color D, knit.

Drop Color D.

[Repeat Rnds 1–2] 87 times or until Striped Section matches the Color Block Section in length.

Bind off.

Weave in yarn ends. Block scarf.

How to Use This Book

My patterns are very simple to follow, but the following information will be helpful.

Yarn

The yarns for any particular project are what I decided to use and can be substituted to suit your own preferences. In noting the yarn that I have used, you'll see that I indicate the weight of the yarn (sport, DK, medium worsted, super bulky, etc.) and its fiber make-up (100% wool, 70% wool/30% silk, etc.). To get a result that closely resembles what you see in the photo, particularly in regard to drape, you'll want to use a yarn of the same weight and with a similar fiber content.

I've found that a medium worsted-weight #4 cotton yarn may easily substitute for a wool yarn of the same weight. If replacing a silk yarn, try one with a high nylon content to achieve the same delicate drape. Your local yarn store can be a great resource for answering questions about how a yarn will behave in different circumstances.

Yarn is what draws us to this hobby, so be sure to do a little research and choose ones you love and that will achieve the look you want.

Standard Yarn Weight System

Categories of yarn, gauge ranges, and recommended needle and hook sizes

Yarn Weight Symbol & Category Names	0 LACE	1 SUPER FINE	2 FINE	3 LIGHT	4 MEDIUM	5 BULKY	6 SUPER BULKY
Type of Yarns in Category	Fingering 10-count crochet thread	Sock, Fingering, Baby	Sport, Baby	DK, Light Worsted	Worsted, Afghan, Aran	Chunky, Craft, Rug	Bulky, Roving
Knit Gauge Range* in Stockinette Stitch to 4 inches	33–40** sts	27–32 sts	23–26 sts	21–24 st	16–20 sts	12–15 sts	6–11 sts
Recommended Needle in Metric Size Range	1.5–2.25 mm	2.25–3.25 mm	3.25–3.75 mm	3.75–4.5 mm	4.5–5.5 mm	5.5–8 mm	8 mm and larger
Recommended Needle U.S. Size Range	000–1	1 to 3	3 to 5	5 to 7	7 to 9	9 to 11	11 and larger
Crochet Gauge* Ranges in Single Crochet to 4 inches	32–42 double crochets**	21–32 sts	16–20 sts	12–17 sts	11–14 sts	8–11 sts	5–9 sts
Recommended Hook in Metric Size Range	Steel*** 1.6–1.4 mm	2.25–3.5 mm	3.5–4.5 mm	4.5–5.5 mm	5.5–6.5 mm	6.5–9 mm	9 mm and larger
Recommended Hook U.S. Size Range	Steel*** 6, 7, 8 Regular hook B–1	B–1 to E–4	E–4 to 7	7 to I–9	I–9 to K–10 ½	K–10 ½ to M–13	M–13 and larger

* GUIDELINES ONLY: The above reflect the most commonly used gauges and needle or hook sizes for specific yarn categories.

** Lace weight yarns are usually knitted or crocheted on larger needles and hooks to create lacy, openwork patterns. Accordingly, a gauge range is difficult to determine. Always follow the gauge stated in your pattern.

*** Steel crochet hooks are sized differently from regular hooks—the higher the number, the smaller the hook, which is the reverse of regular hook sizing.

This Standards & Guidelines booklet and downloadable symbol artwork are available at: **YarnStandards.com**

beg	beginning		p	purl
BO	bind off		patt	pattern
C4B	slip 2 sts to cable needle and hold to back, knit 2 sts, then knit 2 sts from cable needle		psso	pass slipped st(s) over
			pwise	purlwise
C4F	slip 2 sts to cable needle and hold to front, knit 2 sts, then knit 2 sts from cable needle		RC	Right Cross: Knit into second st on LH needle, knit into first stitch on LH needle, slip both sts onto RH needle
C6F	slip 3 sts to cable needle and hold to front, knit 3 sts, then knit 3 sts from cable needle		rem	remaining
			rep	repeat
C8F	slip 4 sts to cable needle and hold to front, knit 4 sts, then knit 4 sts from cable needle		RH	right hand
			rnd	round
CO	cast on		RS	right side (public side) of fabric
cont	continue		skp	slip 1 st knitwise, knit next st, insert LH needle through front loop of slipped st and pass it over the knit st—1 st dec'd
dec('d)	decrease(d)			
inc('d)	increase(d)			
k	knit		sl	slip
kwise	knitwise		ssk	one at a time, slip the next 2 sts as if to knit. Insert LH needle into fronts of the 2 sts and knit together—1 st dec'd
k2tog	knit 2 sts together—1 st dec'd			
k3tog	knit 3 sts together—2 sts dec'd			
LH	left hand		st(s)	stitch(es)
MB	Make bobble: Make 5 sts in one stitch as follows: [knit in the front, back, front, back, front of same stitch]. TURN. Purl 5. TURN. Knit 5. TURN. Purl 5. TURN. K2tog, k2tog, knit 1, slip first 2 sts over the last st and off the needle, leaving 1 st.		St st	stockinette stitch
			WS	wrong side of fabric
			wyib	with yarn in back
			yo	yarn over

Gauge

We don't all knit to the same standard. Ask two knitters to each knit a square of stockinette 20 stitches by 24 rows, and chances are when you measure the squares, they won't be the same size. That's because of tension, which refers to how tightly or loosely you hold the working yarn as you knit it.

Enter gauge swatches. At the beginning of each pattern, you'll see the gauge for that particular design, for instance, 20 sts x 24 rows in stockinette stitch = 4"/10 cm square. This means, the final measurements indicated for that particular piece are based on this gauge. If you knit a swatch and it doesn't match up with the gauge, you can adjust your gauge by going to a smaller or larger needle. If your swatch has more stitches and rows than it should, move to progressively larger needles until you hit gauge. If it has fewer, move to progressively smaller needles. The good news is that with scarves, gauge is much less critical that it is when making a sweater.

Blocking

At the end of many of my patterns, you will see the direction to block the piece. Blocking helps relax and even out your knitted stitches for a finished, professional look. Blocking only works with natural fibers, and it's not necessary with every piece. If you finish knitting a scarf and like the look of it as is, you're good to go. But if you finish it and it's looking decidedly homemade, try blocking the piece. The results can be amazing.

1. You will need a bowl, some wool wash (I like Soak), and two large towels.

2. Add the finished scarf and a few drops of wool wash to the bowl and fill with cool water.

3. Submerge the scarf and *gently* swish it around to release any air bubbles; you want it to become fully saturated. Let the scarf soak for about 15 to 20 minutes.

4. Drain the water from the bowl. Do not squeeze or wring your scarf! It looks pretty pathetic at this point, but that's okay. It will recover!

5. Carefully arrange the scarf on a towel. Be sure not to pull or tug on any one part of your scarf.

(continued)

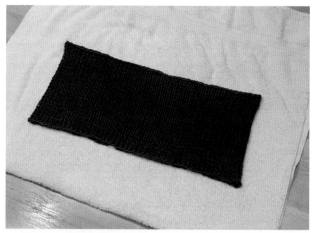

6. Roll the scarf up in the towel, gently pressing and squeezing to get as much water out of the scarf as you can.

7. Unroll the towel and check on your scarf. Lay it flat on the other, dry towel. Gently arrange it the way you would like it to dry. Line up your stitches, smooth out any bumps, then leave it to dry completely, which will take about one day. Do not touch it until it's dry! You can repeat this process as many times as you want to get the stitches just the way you want them.

Techniques & Stitches

For your convenience, I've included tutorials for the techniques and stitches used in my patterns that might be less familiar to knitters. Also remember that the internet is a great source for knitting technique videos, if I haven't included a tutorial for stitch you might want a refresher on.

Joining to Work in the Round

Joining your cast-on stitches to work in the round is the key to this book. Take care to follow these steps to get started!

1. Using the cast-on of your choosing and a circular needle, cast on the required number of stitches for the pattern.

2. Lay the needle flat and check that the stitches are all facing in the same direction and are not twisted over the needle.

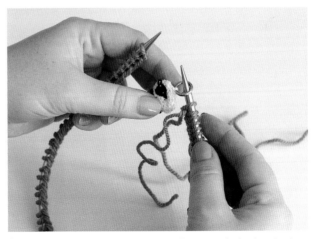

3. Slip a stitch marker on the needle to mark the beginning of the round.

(continued)

4. Begin knitting into the first stitch with the working yarn. Be sure you don't grab the tail by mistake!

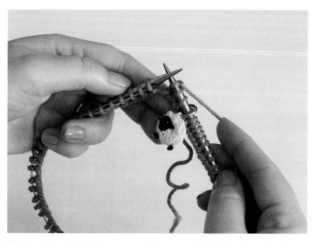

5. Continue knitting around the needle. You're knitting in the round! When you knit all the stitches simply slip the stitch marker from the LH needle to the RH needle and continue knitting.

Cable Cast-On

The Cable Cast-On can be used as the main cast-on for your projects but it is also used as in the Picot Cast-On and Picot Bind-off.

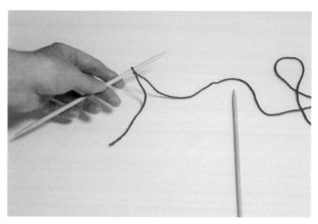

1. Begin with a slip knot on the needle.

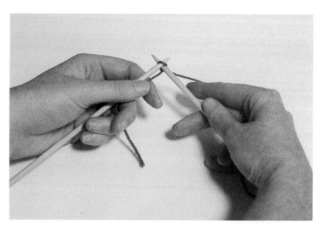

2. Knit into the first stitch.

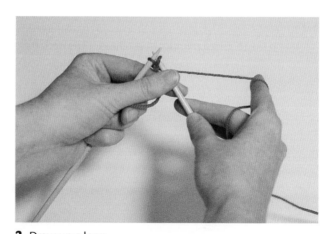

3. Draw up a loop.

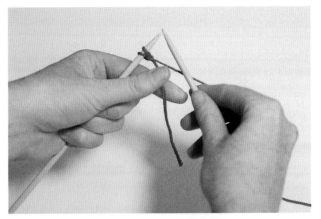

4. Slip the new loop from the RH needle back to the LH needle.

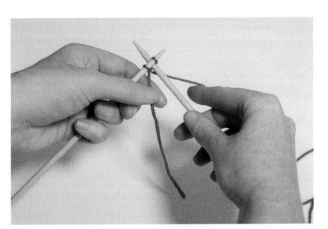

5. For the second stitch and all remaining stitches, insert the RH needle between the last 2 stitches on the LH needle.

6. Draw up a loop and slip loop back to LH needle.

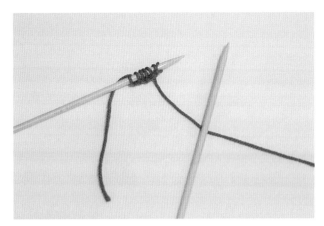

7. Repeat for required number of stitches.

Picot Cast-On

Adding small picot stitches to a cast-on makes for a decorative edge. You will use a Cable Cast-On for this.

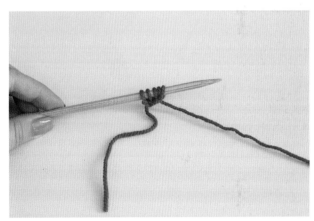

1. Using the Cable Cast-On, cast on 5 stitches.

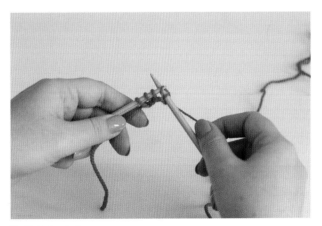

2. Knit 2 stitches.

(continued)

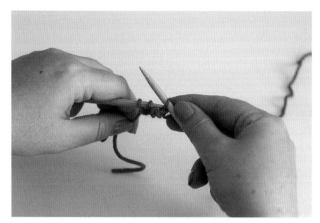

3. Bind off 2 stitches.

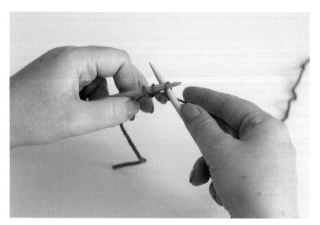

4. Cast on 4 stitches

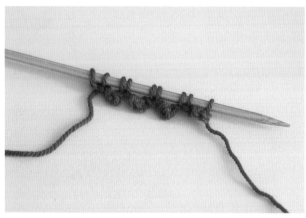

5. Repeat Steps 2–4 until required number of stitches are on the needle.

Picot Bind-Off

This bind-off takes a bit longer than a usual bind-off but the decorative edge is worth the extra time. Again, this makes use of the Cable Cast-On.

1. Using the Cable Cast-On, cast on 2 stitches.

2. Bind off 5 stitches.

3. Slip the last stitch back onto the LH needle; repeat Steps 1–3 around.

Cables

Knit right-twisting and left-twisting cables by simply holding the stitches to the front (cable will twist right) or back (cable will twist left) of the work. You can make cables larger or smaller by changing the number of stitches that are held on the cable needle.

Right-Twisting 4-Stitch Cable (C4F)

1. Slip 2 stitches to a cable needle.

2. Hold the cable needle to the front of the work.

3. Knit 2 stitches from the LH needle.

4. Knit 2 stitches held on the cable needle.

(continued)

The cable is complete.

3. Knit 2 stitches from the LH needle.

Left-Twisting 4-Stitch Cable (C4B)

1. Slip 2 stitches to the cable needle.

4. Knit 2 stitches held on the cable needle.

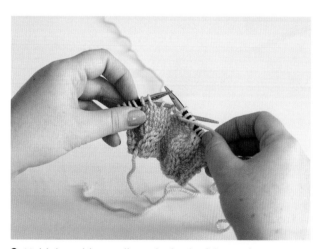

2. Hold the cable needle to the back of the work.

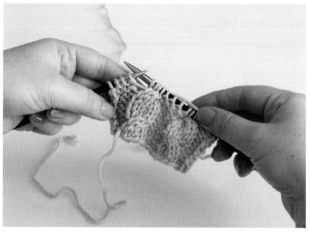

The cable is complete.

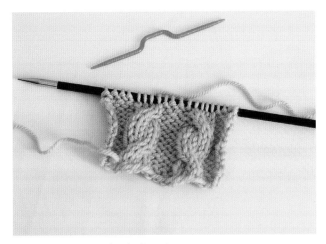

A cable twisting in both directions

Right Cross (RC)

Also called a mock cable, the Right Cross twists two stitches without need of a cable needle. It's a fun stitch to work!

1. Knit into the second stitch on the LH needle.

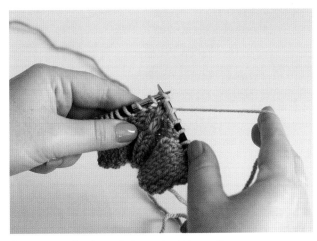

2. Knit into the first stitch on the LH needle.

3. Slip both stitches onto the RH needle.

The right cross is complete.

Bobbles

When you make a bobble, you're stuffing a bunch of stitches and rows into the space of a single stitch.

1. Make 5 stitches in 1 stitch as shown left and above. Knit in the front, back, front, back, and front of the same stitch.

2. *Turn.* Purl 5. *Turn.*

3. Knit 5. *Turn.* Purl 5. *Turn.*

4. K2tog, k2tog, knit 1.

5. Slip the first 2 stitches over the last stitch and off the needle, leaving one stitch.

The bobble is complete.

Double Yarn Over (double yo)

This double-wrap makes a larger eyelet than the traditional yarn over.

1. Approach the position in the pattern requiring a double yo.

2. Yarn over the needle as normal.

3. Wrap yarn around RH needle a second time.

Stranded Knitting

Knitting with two colors is easier than it seems. Try this technique of holding one color in each hand and changing them systematically as the pattern requires.

1. Hold one color in each hand.

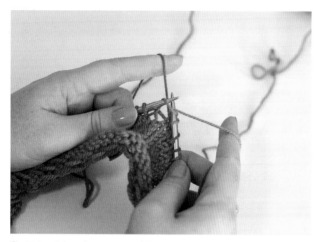

2. Knit with color required by the pattern.

3. Knit with the other color required by the pattern.

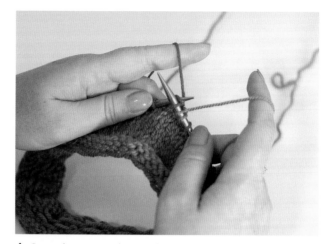

4. Carry the nonworking color with an even tension behind the working color.

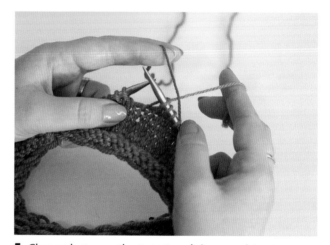

5. Change between the two strands in a consistent manner such as Color A over and Color B under; this will keep the strands from tangling and will prevent gaps from forming in the fabric where the color changes occur

6. From the inside of the work, the yarns should sit with an even tension. If the stitches are pulling or the work looks puckered, try to carry the yarns more loosely. If the stitches appear too loose at the color change, try to add a bit more tension when switching between colors.

Provisional Cast-On

Use this cast-on to begin a project when you want to seamlessly graft the ends together.

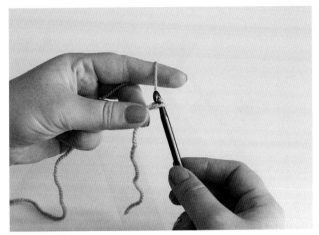

1. With a length of waste yarn, preferably a smooth yarn in a weight similar to your working yarn, and a crochet hook, make a slip knot.

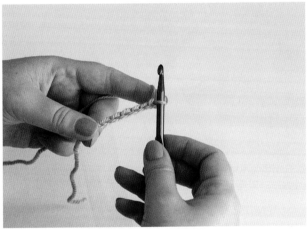

2. Chain the required number of stitches for your selected pattern. Then chain 4 to 6 additional stitches.

3. Cut the waste yarn and finish off the chain.

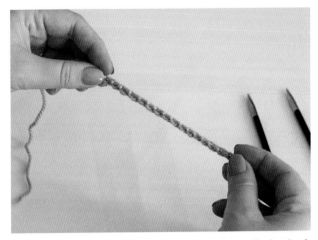

4. Turn the chain over to reveal the "bumps" on the back of the chain.

5. With the working yarn and needle required for the pattern, insert the needle through the first chain bump and wrap the working yarn around the needle.

(continued)

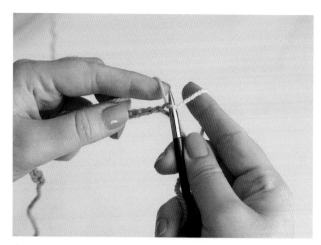

6. Pull the working yarn through the chain and onto the needle—1 st picked up (cast on).

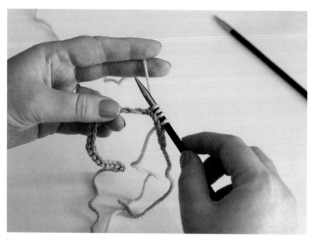

7. Repeat across the chain until you have picked up (cast on) the required number of stitches for your pattern.

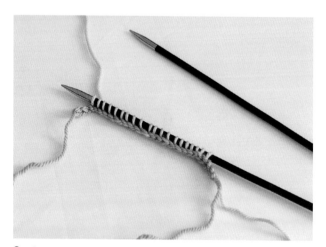

8. The provisional cast-on is complete and you can continue working on the pattern.

To graft one end of a piece to another, you need to remove the waste yarn to release the live stitches, which are transferred to a needle.

1. Release the finishing knot at the end of the crochet chain.

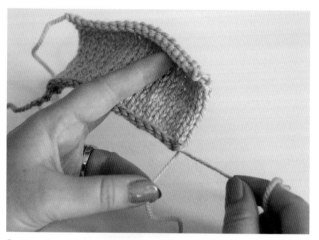

2. Gently undo any chains until you reach the first knit stitch.

3. Insert the knitting needle into the knit stitch and gently pull out the waste yarn.

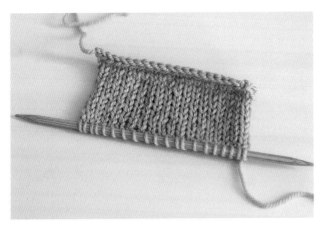

4. Repeat across the row until all knit stitches have been captured on the knitting needle. Discard waste yarn.

Kitchener Stitch

Use the Kitchener Stitch to seamlessly graft the ends of a finished scarf together to create a loop.

1. Align the stitches to be grafted together evenly on two needles. Thread a yarn needle with the tail from one of the ends. You are now ready to begin the Kitchener Stitch. (The example is shown with a contrasting color of yarn as the tail so that the stitches will stand out.)

2. Insert the needle into the first stitch on the FRONT needle as if to PURL. Gently pull the yarn through the stitch, leaving the stitch on the front needle.

3. Insert the needle into the first stitch on the BACK needle as if to KNIT. Gently pull the yarn through the stitch, leaving the stitch on the back needle.

4. Insert the needle into the first stitch on the FRONT needle as if to KNIT. Gently pull the yarn through the stitch and off the front needle.

(continued)

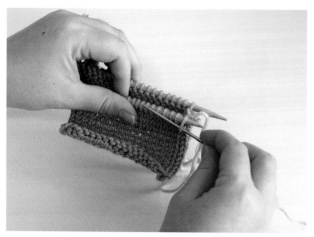

5. Insert the needle through the first stitch on the FRONT needle as if to PURL. Gently pull the yarn through the stitch, leaving it on the front needle.

8. Repeat Steps 4–7 until all the stitches have been worked. If you don't get it on the first try that's ok! Working the Kitchener Stitch takes practice and time. It's a strange technique to graft live stitches together with a yarn needle. Just remember not to pull the stitches too tight with every step—you're adding a new row of knitting, not making a seam.

6. Insert the needle into the first stitch on the BACK needle as if to PURL. Gently pull the yarn through the stitch and off the front needle.

9. Secure your last stitch and weave in your yarn end.

7. Insert the needle into the first stitch on the BACK needle as if to KNIT. Gently pull the yarn through the stitch leaving it on the back needle.

Yarn Sources

The yarns used in this book are some of my favorites!
You'll find them at a variety of craft stores and boutique yarn shops.

Artyarns
www.artyarns.com

Blue Sky Alpacas
www.blueskyalpacas.com

Ewe Ewe Yarns
www.eweewe.com

Fairmount Fibers, distributors of Manos del Uruguay
www.fairmountfibers.com

Freia Fibers
www.freiafibers.com

RYN Yarns, distributors of Kauni
www.rynyarn.com

Knit Collage
www.knitcollage.com

Lion Brand
www.lionbrand.com

Plymouth Yarn
www.plymouthyarn.com

Tahki Stacy Charles
www.tahkistacycharles.com

Skacel Collection
www.skacelknitting.com

Spud & Chloë
www.spudandchloe.com

Yarns of Rhichard Devrieze
www.rdyarns.com

Visual Index

Super Simple Cowl

2

Color Pop Cowl

5

Del Mar Derby Wrap

8

Date Night Infinity Loop

11

Sea Glass Cowl

15

Adorned

18

Basket Case Infinity Scarf

21

A Touch of Glitter Cowl

26

Save the Sunset Neck Warmer

30

Beach Break Loop

33

Changing Tides Cowl

36

Seaside Lace Capelet

39

High Speed Cable Cowl

44

Sweater Weather Scarf

47

Tangerine Twist

50

Double Agent Wrap

53

Popcorn & Purls

57

Entrelac Effect Neck Warmer

60

Pixel Perfect

66

Desert Dreams
69

Snow Drifter Scarf
72

Blue Lagoon Infinity Scarf
76

The Harlequins
79

Pretty Preppy
82

Color Block Scarf
85

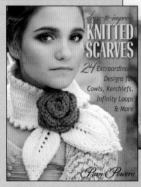